PRAISE FOR *HEARD-HOARD*

Winner of the Alice Fay di Castagnola Award from the Poetry Society of America

Finalist, PEN America's Voelcker Poetry Award

Boston Globe Best Books of the Year

"A superb book about people attempting to make a life together in America. . . . This book is crucial to contemporary American poetry because it shows a lyric poet of unique formal gifts doing something we'd usually expect from a great novelist— exploring and rendering our striving to give shape and meaning to our lives together— all while maintaining the force and subtlety of his lyric gift."

—PETER CAMPION, *Adroit Journal*

"The stakes here are extraordinarily high: salvation, protection, soul-fashioning. . . . Riley is like a painter who increasingly allows color, form, and texture to be his guide in creating universal sensory, emotional, and philosophical effects. . . . In these pages, he creates a uniquely American idiom—expressive, earthy, and flat-out dazzling."

—JULIAN GEWIRTZ, *World Literature Today*

"In ways that few poets can access—think Hopkins, Celan—Riley is at work in a different intelligence language holds, one folded underneath the ratios of daily logic. . . . We gain permission to enter a sacred and strange field, where words don't describe a life, but a life is inscribed in words."   —DAN BEACHY-QUICK, *Colorado Review*

"Linguistically and sonically intense, emotionally buffeting. . . . I can't think of a poet writing now more original, more true to his internal tuning fork and singular vision."   —CAROL MOLDAW, *Lana Turner*

"Disquietingly original. . . . Radical in its bracing mix of lyric and narrative and in its deeply compassionate humanism."   —MEG SCHOERKE, *Hudson Review*

"A poet perpetually at the top of his craft, balancing music and silence to create power. . . . Like Faulkner's Yoknapatawpha County, Riley's South Carolina lowcountry is surely part reality, part fiction—and one hundred percent truth."

—EMILY PÉREZ, *Georgia Review*

"The strongest new book of poetry this year. . . . One of the most exciting books of poetry I've read in my life."   —*Bookworm's* Top Ten Books of 2021

"No one in American poetry has a voicebox quite like Atsuro Riley's."

—*Boston Globe's* Best Books of 2021

"Haunting. . . . Riley's oeuvre breaks new lyric ground with its singular style. This rich, polyphonic collection will keep readers entranced."   —*Publishers Weekly*

"The collection calls us back to the roots of language, breaking it apart and putting it back together."   —LINDSAY WEISHAR, *Ploughshares*

"Riley splits words apart and arranges them in counterpoint to create a singular music, an effect like cracking open a geode to reveal its secret inner glittering. Readers will enter a fully-formed world, with its own characters, myths, chorus, and repetitions. Sonically and emotionally complex."

—KATHERINE LITWIN, Poetry Foundation's Library Book Picks

"Lush and strange, Riley's voice is utterly transfixing. . . . His vision is rich with luminous lines."   —MAYA POPA

HEARD-HOARD

HEARD-HOARD

ATSURO RILEY

The University of Chicago Press

Chicago and London

The University of Chicago Press, Chicago 60637
The University of Chicago Press, Ltd., London
© 2021 by The University of Chicago
Published 2021
Paperback edition 2024
Printed in the United States of America

33 32 31 30 29 28 27 26 25 24   1 2 3 4 5

ISBN-13: 978-0-226-78942-2 (cloth)
ISBN-13: 978-0-226-83337-8 (paper)
ISBN-13: 978-0-226-78956-9 (e-book)
DOI: https://doi.org/10.7208/chicago/9780226789569.001.0001

Cover illustration: Anonymous, "Untitled" (2008) (detail). Udaipur,
Rajasthan, India. From *Tantra Song: Tantric Painting from Rajasthan*,
edited by Franck André Jamme (Catskill, NY: Siglio, 2011).

Library of Congress Cataloging-in-Publication Data

Names: Riley, Atsuro, author.
Title: Heard-hoard / Atsuro Riley.
Description: Chicago : University of Chicago Press, 2021. | Includes
    bibliographical references.
Identifiers: LCCN 2021007909 | ISBN 9780226789422 (cloth) | ISBN
    9780226789569 (ebook)
Subjects: LCGFT: Poetry.
Classification: LCC PS3618.I5326 H43 2021 | DDC 812/.5—dc24
LC record available at https://lccn.loc.gov/2021007909

For Benjamin Davidson

CONTENTS

HEARD-HOARD

CRACKLER

What came to seem to him the core

(the pulsing core)

is wefted, warped: a lit

meat-mesh of heards

What tales he'd gnawed like seeds like sparks

live ember-words

(lucernal core)

—red (gold) filaments sting and thrum

CALL

It starts with the lamp that lamped our night our dirt.

Cause of this (wear-balded) red-mud ring going glow.

The old ever-voice (with the tear through it) intonating, rivering.

Souls and appetites (from holler, brink, and gully) lured and drawn.

The story-man encircling us binding us by lard-torch and ditty.

So.

In the beginning.

And it came to pass.

Wait'll I tell you.

Tale-flicker from his crackling throat; blackening (kerosened) cattail held high:

—Some say what she'd gripped right then wadn't vine but bullsnake.

—Hadn't they clung tooth and claw to branch and bark.

—When the creekbend child got beat got hided fresh his mama broke her switch.

—Damned if dog-daisies beanstalks didn't fank up in the spokes.

Our pulse.

Our (crescendo-timbrous) amphi-glade of bug-chirk, burgeon.

Well was it green as this ever.

Bright breath of the lamp that lamps our night.

(Our dirt.)

SUNDER

A last rock-skip hurlstorm (crazing river-glass)
the closest they ever were.

•

In right lockstitch
snared and split some fire-supper cooked on sticks.

•

By dawn the older brother took to chucking
what bottle-frags he could find and crud-oysters across.
The (high-pitched) younger blacked our waters

with a yowl.

•

Lord the sound such as rose from him

carried so—

Carved

into us. Clings.

•

Hadn't they clung tooth and claw to branch and bark.

—Came a man (and truck) to take them off.

•

Dieseled those boys off

away

some say somewheres upcountry,

inland.

•

Where it was they landed (why) nobody not them knows.

•

No body not them knows

just how they humped and grubbled home

what road they'd graved what woods crisscrossed

which creeks which trains they'd hopped who helped.

•

Came safe home sure   *but blank as houses.*

Came safe home   —as him. —and him.

—as (evermore) not them.

SHED

—But roughly but adequately it can shelter

In which she whomped
and tamped the earth to make a floor.

Beat a rhythm-rain
of brunts with oar and haft.

Gagged raw wallboards
(gaps and cracks) with chiggermoss with oyster-sacks.

Would some nights leak
a howl.

Rough-rigged a roof
(*some type of sail?*) from linoleum-scrimp and plastic.

Hacked a (splintery) hole
but hung no door.

Through which I'm put
more nights than not—*Could I be the flickering in her structure.*

Would some nights leak

a howl (a count) a whistling-through.

I'm coiled inside

this shape she wracked and made.

STRIPLINGS

[field]

Truck a passel (a poke) of wildling boys

We call ourselves (our pack) the pickup-slaves

Upcountry— loosed from mothers

Farmed out for scratch by mamas

Pale (pink-backed) tobacco-crew

Bossed by peeled-stick (breakback) donkey-switch

Tarred cropper-force

Forced cropper-line

Right far afield past Social Knob

Dark welty field near Luris

[bunkhouse]

Most nights the boy they called Tynan

suppered us with scrapple from a can. Or some black-eyes

he'd've road-begged; a quarter-peck of crowders

scrounged off vines.

     •

The broad back-skin on the tallest boy

  —a (ripening) welt-weave, a lattice.

     •

Last good gloam-minute after work

we'd strip off there in the side-yard, yawping; taking turns

de-tarring   un-burning

arc-aiming cool hose-spray each on each.

     •

Eleven of us / *chigger-scritches, scablets.*

Eleven of us / *none of us clean.*

•

Where the boss of us bore down

on us   our rank of bedrolls on the floorboards   one

and one and one *eleven of us*   ranked sack-beds

on floorboards   boots of   black breath of   the boss

•

of us bearing down on us—

ain't none of us (not a one of us) clean.

[after-road]

And so the (heaving) boys got yoked and dragged

toward CANDY'S STOP

•

up Hwy. 52 one night

and dumped.

CHORUS: *Petition*

Dear

Green

Encompass us

'Where springs not fail'

Canes not break nor welt on backs of leg

Fresh cresses plait

Where no plaque of heated iron scathes

(Nor epithet

Nor noose nor knives)

Let

Articulated scapes arise

MOTH

I been 'Candy' since I came here young.

My born name keeps but I don't say.

To her who my mama was I was
pure millstone, cumbrance. *Child ain't but a towsack full of bane.*

Well I lit out right quick.

Hitched, and so forth. Legged it.
Was rid.

Accabee at first (then, thicket-hid) then Wadmalaw;
out to Nash's meat-yard, Obie's jook. At
County Home they had this jazzhorn drumbeat
orphan-band 'THEM LAMBS' they—

They let me bide and listen.

This gristly man he came he buttered me
then took me off (swore I was surely something) let me ride in back.

Some *thing*—

(snared) (spat-on) Thing

being morelike moresoever what he meant.

No I'd never sound what brunts he called me what he done

had I a hundred mouths.

How his mouth. Repeats

on me down the years. Everlastingly

riveled-looking, like rotfruit. Wasn't it

runched up like a grub.

First chance I inched off (back through bindweed) I was gone.

Nothing wrong with *gone* as a place

for living. Whereby a spore eats air when she has to;

where I've fairly much clung for peace.

Came the day I came here young

I mothed

my self. I cleaved apart.

A soul can hide like moth on bark.

My born name keeps but I don't say.

CREEKTHROAT

—We seen his mama she dry and scant

By hook or by bent
I guttle the rudimental stories.

I'm all in-scoop
suck and swallow by dint of birth. Of shape.

—Were *you* hallow-nursed on riversource
upon a time (or ' *the rocky breasts forever* ') I was not.

I learned to lie in want
for succor-food; for forms; I gaped I gulped for what I got.

Nowadays to need
to come by what comes by here comes natural and needs no bait.

Just steep dead-still as a blacksnake
creek and wait.
          [*my chokesome weeds, my crook, my lack, my epiphytes, my cypress knees ...*]

This old appetite as chronic as tides—
on foot or by boat by night (*please*) come slake me with radicle stories.

DUET

—But that that brace of brothers pleached a song

Had we voice *!*

a voice

a braid-reed voice

our good throats restored

(our lockstitch chord)

We would

croodle-keen

(could breathe)

our lodged our

locked unsaids—

Duet our not-thought knowns—

•

That this fear-axe weighs caustic on the walls of the mind.

That it gibbet-looms over us gleam-breathing pendulating all the time fixing to fall.

That a body gets (a soul gets) fostered same by beauty sure by fear.

That sure as fangs a threat-pestered sheeny cottonmouth gon' gape.

That this whip-shape underfoot in pinestraw: more a diamondback turned flinchy.

That the (leaf-crinching) coldcoiled copperheads will spring.

That once upon a switchblade spring a man a crudded truck coerced us off.

That the annals they will show how young and green.

That a snappin' turtle's jawbeak (puncts you like a bear-trap) stays sunk in meat till lightning.

That some are bent to hunt to use a thing or eat or crush it since they can.

That we ourselves would kick-dent and axe-batter any innocent flank of galvanize for noise.

That anyhow trust the skinny scenthounds to backtrack more or less their track to home exactly.

That our mother salt-saves food for the end of the world.

CLARY

Her cart like a dugout canoe.

Had been an oak trunk.

Cut young.   Fire-scoured.

What was bark what was heartwood: *Pure Char-Hole*

Adze-hacked and gouged.

Ever after (never not) wheeling hollow there behind her.

Up the hill toward Bennett Yard; down through Eight-Mile, the Narrows.

Comes Clary by here now

Body bent past bent.   Intent upon horizon and carry.

Her null eye long since gone isinglassy, opal.

—The potent (brimming, fluent) one looks brown.

Courses Clary sure as bayou through here now

Bearing (and borne ahead by) hull and hold behind her.

Plies the dark.

Whole nights most nights along the overpass over Accabee.

Crosses Clary bless her barrow up there now

Pausing and voweling there—

                              the place where the girl fell.

(   )

Afterwhile passing.

Comes her cart like a whole note held.

CHORUS: *Lobe*

The coarse croker-sack cloth

she'd grown to clutch

mesh-merged with her

woof and pang

swole to serve

more like organ

than protection

STRANGER

They would congregate right regular.

  •

(In the dirt-lot of the First Baptist
or along by that abattoir off the brackcreek.)

  •

The hot meat of the matter
being to parse-patch what they'd heard of what she was.

  •

Marrowwise what she was to them was
foreign-faced *Not natural : Not from here.*

  •

Of no (known) rhizomatic strain nor kith nor kin.

•

Word said and word'd spread *She's some flotsam*
from that load of 'those' what flooded here by boat.

•

Say they bought some bait from off her cart—
how they'd pincer-snatch their change like she was hot.

•

—pink dew-worms I got! fish-eyes & roaches. live
minnows for cheap. chicken (neck) gristle. no crickets.

•

Her (uncreased) neck her every body-part their snack.

•

Theirs to eyeball-eat and memorize;
to judge; to pass from each to each from mouth to ear.

•

Have you smelled the hair on her. Have you
bagged a feel of leg. Would you—

•

You could always put a bag on her. Why she all the time
bansheeing (bent down) dawn-sweeping her dirt.

•

Possessed by slingstone fireball-bags of shit they torched her yard.

•

(Wouldn't they congregate
right regular.)

•

By time and ire her rent-house formed a skin of dunt and char.

CAW

Whose branch this is I think you know.

By how my (question-marks as) claws inscritch the bark.

How my worry-work along this bough

runs back and forth (and copper-keen) and evermore;

I got mocked and nicked *No-Fly Bird*

not for nothing.

Not for nothing have I picked this oak.

Though not thicktrunk-ancient as some angel-oak,

it's sure the highest of our high so suits my lack.

—Charred wings won't lift; I've got no glide

nor span to speak of. *Ain't this my beat : my usual limb.*

Ain't this pecking (carking) pulse

my far and wide.

CRAW

Split the boy—   his thorax, throat
Pierce-peel the craw:

A jag-crystalled crust—   his black scoria, slag
(Not *'Bulb after Bulb, in Silver rolled'*)

What no gizzard ground (could hope to grind)
What will not mesh
What will not smelt

Embedded undigested there in meat

GOLDHOUND

The old master (kneeling)

mastered me

gave good and goad

would hie me forth

(unsnicked my choke-chain)

sicced me loose—

'*Go birddog you some marvels*'

•

[reaping]

Dew-sparks galaxifying

the crabgrass the spurgeweed

(back of her house).

•

Ain't everybody cross the universe

knowin : her baitworms

is pink and prime.

•

But (rose-fingered) righteous

as this hour is—*But where*

on god's good green they at.

•

(Ought not there to be umpteen scrawlers

here scrawling.) *Bout now they*

supposed to show thick on the ground.

•

Wait—that flashlight

fret-crossing (nerve-raking) the matted turf

means the wormmonger they call Willa.

•

Crash of ransack; *her frenzies.*

Couldn't Willa's raccoon-rooting (mongst the

woodshed toolpile) mean a plan has dawned.

•

By and by her zigzag contraption-rig

will ramify here and crackle. For all the world

a thrum-web of (splice-splayed) electric cords & tree-lights

•

raw-wired to butterknives

screwdrivers   shirt-hangers

stakes.

•

Stake your scrag of ground with what you've got.

Drag the hose (from front around to back) to soak the earth.

Plug in all the prongs to call the juice : to light the dirt to wreathe the oak.

O Willa : watch your (writhing) living rise to shine.

[heard, at Nash's]

'It ain't no kind of Love

unless you get some of it on you . . . '

[instrumental]

Why does the swimhole marsh-meander sound like drums like guns like thunder.

Why this particular articulate pulse.

Why does the boy wrangle-drag and poise this cankery scrapsheet of galvanize.

Why his battering limb and throe and pang.

[cottage-work]

Along the

weed-embrangling snuffle-path

down through Eight-Mile

the Narrows

The pure

is-ness

of Necessity

carrying on—

•

Off this horse-trailer hid by coppervines you can buy yourself
a pussy or a pecker—picture of. *Which you wantin* the only
question. Or *how many*. Razor-exacted out of magazines;
tendered neat in baggies—or waxed paper—clean as stamps.

•

This long grove here you can pick from—a ripe olio

of (vacated) wasp-houses

hung like lamps.

•

Revival's on offer in this glow-field — *ETERN'LY OPEN!*—

flush with loud-painted

Jesus-fluent gourds.

•

Word says—renting that stripped-wood A-frame yonder is a

new woman nobody knows. How she'll scald and scour out

quick *all your bringings in her bathtub*—your miles of pig-guts

(for the chitlin strut, the ᴘiney supper) bundled spruce as

laundry.

•

And there behind GreenHaven the Myrtises

will sell you a word.

For curse or for cure

or they'll salt some through your letters.

•

Mr. W. being known

for fine-carving these stern pine-paddles

(fresh-hewn for use by fathers).

Known to sear to scar.

•

Under the last loved legs of this cinder-bridge the *Boat Lady* (name of Zindi) floats and hoards. The original *woodboat what brung her* evermore propagating here like spatterdock—new boatlet-rooms as her need grows; slapdashed out of scrap; lashed together another unto another. Don't we all of us reckon Zindi harbors one kind of everything on her hodgepodge shelves. Be it seedpod or radicle or shark's tooth; dry sloughskin or chasmal ribcage or jaw. *Come look—Do I look like I'm needin your cash moneys.* Be it barter (something) or browse.

[river]

The bare

(brindling)

word of it

Word enough—

CHORUS: *Milk*

His mother

came (she said) from salt

so fed him salt.

Raised to wolf

white roots and dirt

she fed him dirt.

ORIGIN

[Tetsu-san schools her son]

Bloomed no intention not no notion

       of a child but out you came.

What some got natural mothery

       know-to-do unborn in me.

I been brought from cross the water far—

       every bone a alien never not.

(No soil no roots yall clinch so hard

       for home gon' be my home.)

My flint mama was no lamp to me

       nor well my name she gave means iron.

Long nights back home we boiled our sea

       for salt to sell the salt.

On me mongst moss and spruce the uncles

and the *sofu* took their turns.

Time and tide I'd had to burn

to (cauldron) boil the sea and eat the salt.

Himself who was your seed he called me

Steel when he would call me liked my sharp.

Yes once you heard him down the

telephone (some breaths) the line broke off—

RHYTHM

The time she bent to eat our dirt

The cane-pole threshed her spine.

Times I was made to bend to eat red mud (our dirt) her cane-pole threshed my spine.

CHORUS: *Seed*

The knee-boy

bent to his daddy's shoes

spit-gobbetting and rag-shammying

hard for shine.

ELEMENT

— *the exactest element for us,*
In which we pronounce joy like a word of our own

Well we'd heard it to be veiny with cottonmouths I'm not gonna lie.

•

For true

the sheer (snake-electric) back-beyond of the place

put a pull on us like a magnet.

•

That that rag-rope (flagged and) barred the path just egged us on.

•

(To go and

skulk- and sidle-learn

to palp and tap the edge

to crack us in.)

•

—What'd we feel there once we'd crossed?

    •

Veritable
thought-thick trunks
of swampfoot oaks.

    •

Something like *'A shift in the structure of experience.'*

    •

Here was
Johnny Pep (shrapped home from war)
branch-dragging
agglomerating discards and disjecta.

    •

His craving wove a plexus (more a house) from limbs and leaves.

·

He knit us in:

he left us be. He let us watch he watched us try

(to climb to ape his crisscross weave)

to pitch to plait the roof.

·

Something like ' *Yall strayboys welcome to be welcome if you work.* '

·

Didn't we 'work'—

particular night-hoots (and near-chromatic whistle-riffs) in echo;

beast-likenesses (or bugs)

he whittled live from hickory showed us how.

·

He'd let us

watch him strip and shave

the shagbark bark

to taste (to read) to mull the grain.

•

Something like ' *root-room* ' I reckon. Something like

•

' *When Johnny Pep hitched home from war*

we took to carving (curing) scraplings into shapes. '

CHORUS: *Knell*

We low on daddies hereabouts

The fathers all but gone

Our lack a weight

a shape a drybone lake

By war by

drink by

gun by

drift

The father's all but gone.

OAK

We were all of us empty of its heft and Tammy could tell.

•

Being she herself was (wildling) (loosestrife-weed)
(undaddied) same as us.

•

Flung chaff-motes that we were
she saw to tell us time and time *that yonder oak* its bark and bulk.

•

She harped on it; she rendered. Instilled-
elucidated treeness piece by part.

•

Have I said yet (howsoever she'd've told us) it was never *it* to her but *him*.

•

As in *I school myself I climb the bluff I followfeel the roots of him. They river-*
bound They gnarlin' up from mud [black pluff!] He veins the bank.

•

Some say. Word was.
—That her (fleetblooded) actual daddy jacked the toll-thru (humps the trains).

•

She dwelled on it; she brooded. Elaborated-
fleshed for us especially much his arms.

•

How one mossy brawn-span she favored
had been scathed (engraved along its length) by lightning.

•

How the long-muscled (strict, striated) river-hanging-over one would hold.

•

You could loop a rope there Nearabout the bicep
Whap you up a wide horsehead knot to grip. To ride good Rid fear Let's
not feature no blackflow flowin' down below.

•

Cling strong till your hands numb till your blood goes.
Swing low. You could bellow you could holler while you're at it (Bending with you
not to break) You could set yourself swayin' till kingdom come Till he hears you till

•

he weighs you. You could ring rightful like the tongue of a bell.

LADDER

[Johnny Pep, P.O.W.]

When they flang me down that hole I clawed for home—

When they sealed the seam with clay : sucked roots and ore—

When my gut would grind would groan of lack I 'voked some meat—

When I was blindered underground I seen our creek—

When stench would stain the mind the mind would branch—

When I got stripped & roped to stand for sleep I reined my hoss—

When cane-straps flogged us 'cross the field we'd call a tune—

(When rows of welts (still) grave the mind the mind will climb.)

CHORUS: *Hankerer*

Had it had good tang to it or even a cell's cell of succulence

he'd have squirrelled the day away

to paw and

tongue.

THICKET

—Its juices that have greened my chin

We come gnawed by need on hands and knees.

As a creature (nosing) grubble-seeks a spring.

As bendy-spined as bandy snakes through saltshrub   yaupon   needle-brake.

For darkling green;
for thorn-surround.

This absorbing

quaggy
crample-ground.

Of briar-canes (intervolved with kudzu-mesh) and mold.

Of these convoluted vines we grasp to suck.

To taste the pith—
the lumen   the cell-sap flux.

To try to know

some (soursharp) something about something.

Lumen is as lumen does.

'*A little room for turmoil to grow lucid in.*'

Leafwhelmed in here

where Clary sets her cart-tongue down (and blinks, and craves).
In here where Tynan breathes.

We grasp to suck to taste what light.

Let loose the bale that bows us down.

—Bow down.

NOTES

CALL

"Damned if dog-daisies beanstalks didn't fank up in the spokes" adapts language

from Seamus Heaney's poem "Bann Valley Eclogue."

SHED

The epigraph is taken from Elizabeth Bishop's "The Monument."

STRIPLINGS

POKE: A small sack; a clutch of things (or people).

CROWDERS: Greener-tasting cousins to the black-eyed pea, pretty much rampant

through the Carolina hot months. So-named for the cramped living conditions

within their pods.

CHORUS: Petition

"Where springs not fail" is a quotation from "Heaven-Haven" by Gerard Manley

Hopkins.

MOTH

"Had I a hundred mouths" comes down from Virgil (70 BCE–19 BCE) by way

of William Goyen (1915–1983).

CREEKTHROAT

The phrase "the rocky breasts forever" is drawn from "At the Fishhouses" by Elizabeth Bishop.

RADICLE: The embryonic root of a plant; the rootlike beginning of a nerve or vein; the rudimentary particle of anything; a primary atom or element. Charles and Francis Darwin in *The Power of Movement in Plants* (1880): "It is hardly an exaggeration to say that the tip of the radicle thus endowed [with sensitivity] and having the power of directing the movements of the adjoining parts, acts like the brain of one of the lower animals; the brain being seated within the anterior end of the body, receiving impressions from the sense-organs, and directing the several movements."

DUET

CROODLE: The low faint music of birds (to coo as a dove); the humming of a tune.

CRAW

The poem leans upon Emily Dickinson's poem #861 "Split the Lark" and quotes the line "Bulb after Bulb, in Silver rolled."

ORIGIN

TETSU: Japanese; iron. Also a given name. Usually for boys, sometimes used (with or without suffixes) for girls.

SOFU: Japanese; grandfather.

ELEMENT

The epigraph derives from the Wallace Stevens poem "Of Bright & Blue Birds & the Gala Sun."

The phrase "a shift in the structure of experience" quotes from "The Displaced of Capital" by Anne Winters.

The "root-room" formulation comes from a sonnet by G. M. Hopkins, "My own heart let me more have pity on":

> . . . *call off thoughts awhile*
>
> *Elsewhere; leave comfort root-room; let joy size*

THICKET

The epigraph is drawn from Seamus Heaney's *Sweeney Astray*—his translated version of the medieval Irish work *Buile Suibhne*.

CRAMPLE-GROUND: A patch of woodland where roots, stems, and vines are known to *cramble* (creep along the ground or intertwine underfoot) and are thus trod upon and *trampled*.

"Leafwhelmed" is borrowed from Hopkins's 1888 "Epithalamion."

"A little room for turmoil to grow lucid in" is adapted from Amy Clampitt's poem "Losing Track of Language."

"Let loose the bale that bows us down" adapts a phrase from Benjamin Disraeli's novel *Tancred; or, The New Crusade*.

ACKNOWLEDGMENTS

Grateful acknowledgment is made to the journals in which earlier—and in some cases quite different—versions of this work first appeared:

The Threepenny Review

Kenyon Review

Poetry

A Public Space

The New Republic

The Poetry Review

Free Verse

Riddle Fence

Southern Cultures

Poetry International

"CRACKLER" was originally published as "IN WHICH" in the *Kenyon Review*.

An earlier version of "CREEKTHROAT" was reprinted in *The Mind Has Cliffs of Fall: Poems at the Extremes of Feeling*, edited by Robert Pinsky (W.W. Norton, 2019).

"SHED" was reprinted in the anthology *In the Shape of a Human Body I Am Visiting the Earth: Poems from Far and Wide*, edited by Ilya Kaminsky, Jesse Nathan, and Dominic Luxford (McSweeney's, 2017), and featured on *Poetry Daily*.

"MOTH" was featured in the radio series *Poetry Now*.

"CHORUS: *Petition*" and "CLARY" are excerpted and adapted from the author's 2010 book *Romey's Order* (University of Chicago Press).

The photograph on page five is *Gourds for the Martins: Hale County, Alabama* (Summer 1936) by Walker Evans and was originally published in James Agee's book *Let Us Now Praise Famous Men* (Houghton Mifflin, 1941). Reprinted with permission of the US Library of Congress, Prints & Photographs Division, Farm Security Administration / Office of War Information Collection [Reproduction No. LC-USF342-T01-008169-A].

The photograph on page sixty-one is by Jun Fujita, courtesy of the Graham and Pamela Lee collection.

For their fortifying generosities, the author would like to thank:

The Mrs. Giles Whiting Foundation

The Kingsley & Kate Tufts Awards

The Lannan Foundation

The Library of Congress

The Witter Bynner Foundation

The National Endowment for the Arts

The Poetry Foundation

The Unterberg Poetry Center of the 92nd St. Y

The Poetry Society of America

ABOUT THE AUTHOR

ATSURO RILEY is the author of the poetry collections *Heard-Hoard* (University of Chicago Press, 2021) and *Romey's Order* (University of Chicago Press, 2010).

In 2023 Riley was named a Guggenheim Foundation Fellow and a winner of the Arts and Letters Award in Literature from the American Academy of Arts and Letters.

Heard-Hoard was the winner of the Alice Fay di Castagnola Award from the Poetry Society of America and a finalist for the PEN/Voelcker Poetry Award; it was named to "Best Book of the Year" lists by *The Boston Globe* and *Bookworm*.

Romey's Order received the Whiting Award, the Kate Tufts Discovery Award, *The Believer* Poetry Award, and the Witter Bynner Award from the Library of Congress.

Brought up in the South Carolina lowcountry, Atsuro Riley lives in San Francisco.